It's important to reflect on past events and experiences along with the emotions, feelings, and thoughts that accompanied that time period, so that you can learn and grow from them.

# I AM
# ONE OF A KIND

# What matters most in my life?

_____

_____

_____

_____

_____

_____

_____

_____

_____

_____

_____

_____

_____

_____

# Who am I?  Does anyone really know the real me?

_____

_____

_____

_____

_____

_____

_____

_____

_____

_____

_____

_____

_____

_____

# Am I holding onto something I need to let go of?

_____

_____

_____

_____

_____

_____

_____

_____

_____

_____

_____

_____

_____

_____

# JUST BREATHE...

# What am I scared of?

_____

_____

_____

_____

_____

_____

_____

_____

_____

_____

_____

_____

_____

_____

_____

# If this were the last day of my life, what would my plans be for today?

_____

_____

_____

_____

_____

_____

_____

_____

_____

_____

_____

_____

_____

_____

_____

Is it more important to love,
or be loved?

_____

_____

_____

_____

_____

_____

_____

_____

_____

_____

_____

_____

# I AM READY FOR A CHALLENGE

# Does it really matter what others think of me?

_____

_____

_____

_____

_____

_____

_____

_____

_____

_____

_____

_____

_____

_____

_____

_____

_____

# I AM GOING PLACES!

# To what degree have I actually controlled the course of my life?

_____

_____

_____

_____

_____

_____

_____

_____

_____

_____

_____

_____

_____

# AIM FOR THE CLOUDS!

# What makes me smile?

_____

_____

_____

_____

_____

_____

_____

_____

_____

_____

_____

_____

_____

_____

Write about your first love- whether
it was a person. place. or thing.

_____

_____

_____

_____

_____

_____

_____

_____

_____

_____

_____

_____

_____

_____

# What worries me most about the future?

_____
_____
_____
_____
_____
_____
_____
_____
_____
_____
_____
_____
_____
_____
_____

# Which is worse, failing or never trying?

_____

_____

_____

_____

_____

_____

_____

_____

_____

_____

_____

_____

_____

_____

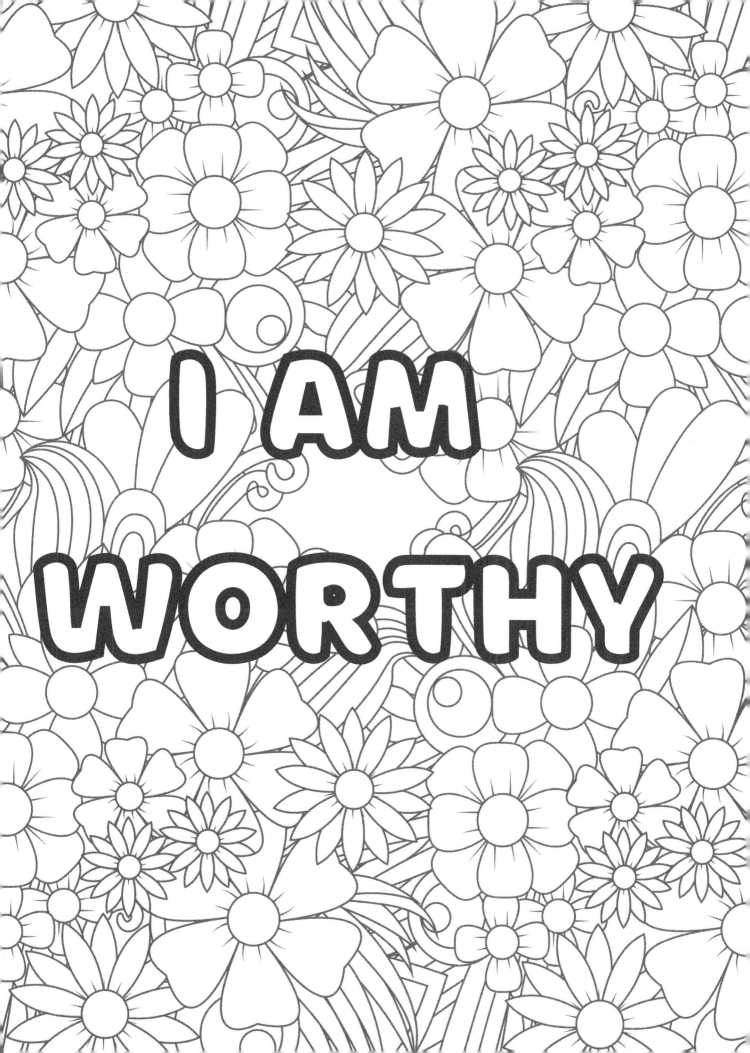

# If my body could talk, it would say...

_____

_____

_____

_____

_____

_____

_____

_____

_____

_____

_____

_____

_____

_____

# What do you wish others knew or understood about you?

_____

_____

_____

_____

_____

_____

_____

_____

_____

_____

_____

_____

_____

_____

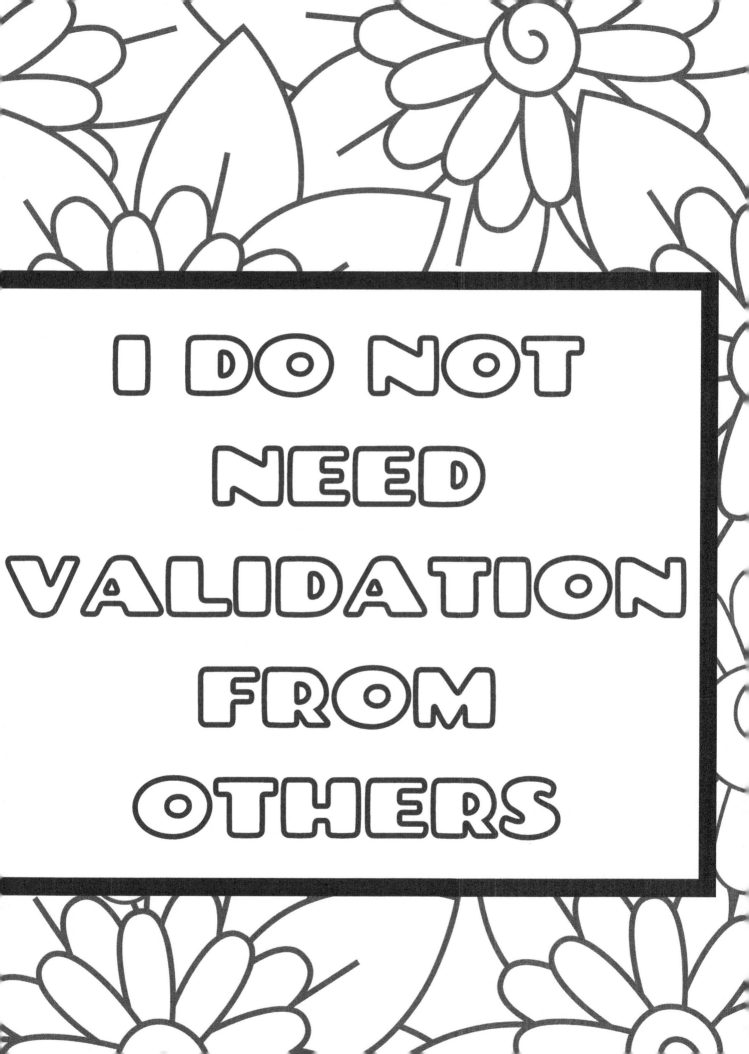

# What have you learned from your biggest mistakes?

_____

_____

_____

_____

_____

_____

_____

_____

_____

_____

_____

_____

_____

_____

_____

_____

# I AM CONFIDENT

Thank you for purchasing this product! I hope you have enjoyed it. Please leave a review on Amazon!

Made in the USA
Coppell, TX
17 February 2023

12971946R00072